THE LIFESTYLE OF PRAYER

But when you pray, go away by yourself, all alone, and shut the door behind you and pray to your Father secretly, and your Father, who knows your secrets, will reward you.

Matthew 6:5

by
Franklin N. Abazie

The Lifestyle of Prayer
COPYRIGHT 2017 BY Franklin N Abazie
ISBN: 978-1-945133-22-0

All right reserved. This book or any portion thereof may not be reproduced or used in any manner whatsoever without the express written permission of the publisher, except for the use of brief quotations in a book review. All Bible quotes are from King James Version and others as noted.

Published by: F N ABAZIE PUBLISHING HOUSE—
aka, Empowerment Bookstore

That I may publish with the voice of thanksgiving and tell of all thy wondrous works.
Psalms 26:7

To order additional copies, wholesales or booking call:
the Church office (973-372-7518)
or Empowerment Bookstore Hotline (973-393-8518)

Worship address:
343 Sanford Avenue, Newark, New Jersey 07106
Administrative Head Office address:
33 Schley Street Newark New Jersey 07112
Email: pastorfranknto@yahoo.com
Website www.fnabaziehealingministries.org
Publishing House: www.fnabaziepublishinghouse.org

This book is a production of F N Abazie Publishing House. A publication Arms of Miracle of God Ministries 2016.

First Edition

CONTENTS

THE MANDATE OF THE COMMISSION......iv
ARMS OF THE COMMISSION......................v
INTRODUCTION......................................vi
CHAPTER 1
What is the Lifestyle of Prayer?.................1
CHAPTER 2
How Does Prayer & Fasting Work?..........23
CHAPTER 3
The Benefit of Prayer & Fasting.................39
CHAPTER 4
Prayer of Salvation....................................80
CHAPTER 5
About the Author......................................91

THE MANDATE OF THE COMMISSION

"The moment is due to impact your world through the revival of the healing & miracle ministry of Jesus Christ of Nazareth.

"I am sending you to restore health unto thee and I will heal thee of thy wounds, said the Lord of Host."

ARMS OF THE COMMISSION

1) F N Abazie Ministries—Miracle of God Ministries (Miracle Chapel Intl)

2) F N Abazie TV Ministries: Global Television Ministry Outreach

3) F N Abazie Radio Ministries: Radio Broadcasting Outreach

4) F N Abazie Publishing House: Book Publication

5) F N Abazie Bible School: also called Word of Healing Bible School (W.O.H.B.S.)

6) F N Abazie Evangelistic Ass: Miracle of God Ministries: Global Crusade

7) Empowerment Bookstore: Book distribution

8) F N Abazie Helping Hands: Meeting the Help of the Needy Worldwide

9) F N Abazie Disaster Recovery Mission: Global Disaster Recovery

10) F N Abazie Prison Ministry: Prison Ministry For All Convicts "Second Chance"

Some of our ministry arms are awaiting the appointed time to commence.

INTRODUCTION

I have always taken prayer as an essential component of life that we must embrace and incorporate into our lifestyle. This is a book inspired by the Holy Spirit to birth a prayer lifestyle out of our life. This book is designed for everyone to learn how to pray.

The effectual fervent prayer of
a righteous man availeth much.
James 5:16

And he spake a parable unto them to this end,
that men ought always to pray, and not to faint.
Luke 18:1

We are commanded to develop a prayer lifestyle if we do not want to fail in life. A lot of us have accomplished a great feat in life, but missed out on their heavenly blessing—not because of sin, but because we failed to develop prayer as a lifestyle.

WHAT IS THE LIFE STYLE OF PRAYER?

The lifestyle of prayer is a disciplined attitude of talking and communicating to God with reverence, respect and honor. It is a way of life for the believer to prove his/her devotion and dedication to God. Often we claim to have a prayer life, but really we do not put it into practice. David prayed three times per day. *"Evening, and morning, and at noon, will I pray, and cry aloud: and he shall hear my voice."* (Psalms 55:17)

The ritual of prayer will increase our faith. In my understanding, there is no way we will develop a lifestyle full of prayer without the manifestation of our faith in God.

Remember...

"But without faith it is impossible to please him: for he that cometh to God must believe that he is, and that he is a rewarder of them that diligently seek him." (Hebrews 11:6) If we must please God we must prove our faith by developing a lifestyle full of persistent prayers.

Hear my prayer, O Lord, and let my cry
come unto thee. Hide not thy face from me
in the day when I am in trouble;
incline thine ear unto me: in the day
when I call answer me speedily.
Psalms 102:1

Our ability to call and receive speedy answers from the throne of God is hidden in the form of covenant keys. There keys are the relevant buttons necessary for us to press in time of need in prayers. Among my greatest interests—besides studying the Bible—is prayer. This book is a nugget that grants us access into the higher realm and deeper things of God.

Let my prayer be set forth before thee
as incense; and the lifting up of my hands
as the evening sacrifice.
Psalms 141:2

John Wesley once said, "God will do nothing on Earth until somebody prays." Until prayer goes up like an incense and the lifting up of our hands as an evening sacrifice, we will forever remain in expectation and anxious for results. *"Hope deferred maketh the heart sick: but when the desire cometh, it is a tree of life."* (Proverbs 13:12)

This publication has been written to help us all apply relevant techniques to bombard heavenly places with strong effective prayer that avails us to God. May the Lord answer all our prayers and grant us support from heaven. May he give us our heart's desires and make all our plans to succeed. Amen.

Happy reading.

HIGHLIGHTS ON STRATEGIES OF WARFARE PRAYERS

WE MUST ALWAYS BEGIN WITH WORSHIP

Every time you worship God, you remind Him that He is a holy God. *"Saying, Holy, holy, holy, Lord God Almighty, which was, and is, and is to come."* (Revelation 4:8) It is written: *"And one cried unto another, and said, Holy, holy, holy, is the Lord of hosts: the whole earth is full of his glory."* (Isaiah 6:3) Worship gets the attention of our angelic host. In worship, we openly proclaim God holy.

WE MUST CONFESS OF OUR SINS AND FORSAKE IT

It is written: *"If we confess our sins, he is faithful and just to forgive us our sins, and to cleanse us from all unrighteousness."* (1 John 1:9)

Sin is the one of the greatest reasons God will not hear our prayer. *"But your iniquities have separated between you and your God, and your sins have hid his face from you, that he will not hear."* (Isaiah 59:2) Unless we confess and forsake our sins, we are not ready to encounter the hand of God through prayer.

For violent offensive warfare prayer to produce results, we must be righteous and cleansed from iniquity. *"Purge me with hyssop, and I shall be clean: wash me, and I shall be whiter than snow."* (Psalms 51:7) It is written: *"Hide thy face from my sins, and blot out all mine iniquities."* (Psalms 51:9)

WE MUST PRAISE HIM SINCERELY FROM THE HEART

Praise is a weapon of warfare. Each time it is deployed diligently, the enemy cannot escape it. *"And when they began to sing and to praise, the Lord set ambushments against the children of Ammon, Moab, and mount Seir, which were come against Judah; and they were smitten."* (2 Chronicles 20:22)

Every time we sincerely praise God, we remind Him that he is great. *"Great is the Lord, and greatly to be praised in the city of our God, in the mountain of his holiness."* (Pslams 48:1)

Remember...

Although praise pleases God, God cannot praise Himself. *"I will praise the name of God with a song, and will magnify him with thanksgiving. This also shall please the Lord better than an ox or bullock that hath horns and hoofs."* (Psalms 69:30-31) We are fearfully and wonderfully made in His image for the most part to think like Him, but loosely we are created to render acceptable praise unto Him.

We are not ready for warfare until our praise level is high enough to provoke angelic intervention. *"Let the high praises of God be in their mouth, and a two-edged sword in their hand; To execute vengeance upon the heathen, and punishments upon the people."* (Psalms 149:5-6)

HIS DESTINY WAS THE CROSS…

HIS PURPOSE WAS LOVE…

HIS REASON WAS YOU…

*And he spake a parable
unto them to this end,
that men ought always to pray,
and not to faint.*

Luke 18:1

Howbeit this kind goeth not out but by prayer and fasting.

Matthew 17:21

PRAYER POINT TO PROVOKE ANGELIC SPEEDY INTERVENTION

1) Father Lord, grant me speed to accomplish greater task in life.

2) Holy Spirit, help me move forward in life, in the name of Jesus.

3) Finger of God, help me recognize my weakness and my strength, in the name of Jesus.

4) Every dark power of confusion in my life, I destroy you, in the name of Jesus.

5) Anointing for constant open heavens, fall on me now, in the name of Jesus.

6) Be destroyed every power assigned to hinder my destiny, in the name of Jesus.

7) God of Abraham, arise and scatter all my enemies, in the name of Jesus.

8) Locate me powers ordained by heaven to make me great, in the name of Jesus.

9) Scatter every hindering blockage placed on my moving forward, in the name of Jesus.

10) Power of God, speak for me this year, in the name of Jesus.

11) Be destroyed strange enemies assigned to afflict my life, in the name of Jesus.

12) I bind the covens of witchcraft powers manipulating my ministry, in the name of Jesus.

13) Catch fire witchcraft money introduced into my life and finances, in the name of Jesus.

14) Catch fire garments of shame and disappointment, in the name of Jesus.

15) I must rise and shine, in the name of Jesus.

16) I must fulfil my calling in life, in the name of Jesus.

17) God arise and use me as a divine showroom to display power and prosperity, in the name of Jesus.

18) Die every triangular power assigned to torment me, in the name of Jesus.

19) Double destruction from heaven, visit every coven speaking against me, in the name of Jesus.

20) Powers of destruction, blow upon my contenders and oppressors, in the name of Jesus.

21) Father Lord, arise and me peace and prosperity in life, in the name of Jesus.

22) Be arrested every dark power and agent of darkness in my life, in the mighty name of Jesus.

23) Let all forces of darkness hindering the movement of God into my life be rendered impotent, in the name of Jesus.

24) Roast by fire every occultism and witchcraft power programmed against me, in the mighty name of Jesus.

25) I must move forward in life, in the name of Jesus.

26) I crush all destiny snatchers and harassers, in the name of Jesus

27) I refuse to quit pursuing my dreams in life, in the name of Jesus.

28) I crush all nightmares and dream harassers, in the name of Jesus.

29) Angelic assistance, help me fulfil my calling, dreams and aspirations, in the name of Jesus.

CHAPTER 1

WHAT IS THE LIFESTYLE OF PRAYER & FASTING?

And he spake a parable unto them to this end that men ought always to pray, and not to faint.
Luke 18:1

Among the signs to know who is a true believer is the ritual and faithfulness to pray to God often. Besides a righteous lifestyle and living a life like Christ Jesus, the act of praying often is crucial. We are commanded to pray as a lifestyle, as defined by the above scripture. We must make the ritual of praying often as a lifestyle. First, we must incorporate prayer into our habit, then into our character and lifestyle.

Loosely defined, the lifestyle of prayer is our ability to develop an everyday prayer life. The lifestyle of prayer is our consciousness to devote and dedicate qualitative time to talk to God privately, as often as possible and for as long as possible. We must discipline ourselves enough—dedicate and devote time to meet with God in prayer. Some folks talk to God only on Sundays, others only when they attend a revival meeting or a Bible study.

We must consciously develop a habit of prayer and fasting to God as often as possible. Besides other fringe benefits of praying often, the lifestyle of prayer reveals our faithfulness to God. It stimulates our faith and encourages us. Most prayer folks do not get scared easily or feel weak and hopeless concerning terror or fear of anything. It is written: *"If God be for us, who can be against us?"* (Romans 8:31)

And this is the confidence that we have in him, that, if we ask any thing according to his will, he heareth us.
1 John 5:14

The lifestyle of prayer and fasting grants us assurance and confidence in life. As believers, we face trials and tribulations in life. We are opposed and contradicted almost by everyone around us. We are the yardstick for others in the society to measure their moral character. The mentality that God answers all our prayers will motivate all of us who love prayer to make fasting and prayer our lifestyle.

Fasting and prayer are the platforms to

Chapter 1   What Is the Lifestyle of Prayer?

be in command over ever-prevailing challenges that confront us in life. In these evil days we are threatened by the wiles and schemes of the devil, agents of darkness is at loose. Some evil forces will not give up on us unless they afflict and torture the lives of believers with evil forces. *"Howbeit this kind goeth not out but by prayer and fasting."* (Matthew 17:21)

For us to develop a prayer life, we must be willing to pray and to fast often. Prayer and fasting is so vital that it grants strength to our spiritual muscles. Just like as physical exercise develops our muscles, prayer and fasting puts strength to our spirits.

> *O thou that hearest prayer,*
> *unto thee shall all flesh come.*
> **Psalms 65:2**

The good news about fasting and prayer is that God records whatever is said by us all at any time. Prayer and fasting humbles us before the Almighty God, who sees inside the secret. Prayer and fasting pull down our flesh, but also lift up our spirit.

Remember…

The devil operates easily with our flesh.

Each time you fast and pray you hinder the devil from arresting your flesh. That is why during prayer and fasting it's easy to get inspiration from the Holy Spirit. It is written: *"For we wrestle not against flesh and blood."* (Ephesians 6:12)

Fasting and prayer are avenues to harmonize our spirit directly with the spirit of God. Speedy answers are guaranteed when we pray and fast. Fasting and prayer accelerate divine intervention from the Holy Ghost. *"Likewise the Spirit also helpeth our infirmities: for we know not what we should pray for as we ought: but the Spirit itself maketh intercession for us with groanings which cannot be uttered."* (Romans 8:26)

Whenever we deprive our body food, we literally humble our spirit man. as we pray during this time, we easily secure the attention of the Holy Spirit. Fasting and prayer bring us into a closer relationship with God.

Our human nature is not built to fast often. We must therefore discipline our flesh if we pray and fasting are to become our lifestyle. Some folks only fast and pray when their pastor or bishop asks them to fast and pray. Others only fast when going for a medical checkup as prescribed by their physician. We must all engraft prayer and fasting as a lifestyle if we are

Chapter 1   What Is the Lifestyle of Prayer?

to make an impact in our lifetime. Prayer and fasting are significant and inevitable for anyone who desires to develop spiritual muscles. We must all learn how to pray and fast.

And it came to pass, that, as he was praying in a certain place, when he ceased, one of his disciples said unto him, Lord, teach us to pray, as John also taught his disciples. And he said unto them, When ye pray, say, Our Father which art in heaven, Hallowed be thy name. Thy kingdom come. Thy will be done, as in heaven, so in earth. Give us day by day our daily bread. And forgive us our sins; for we also forgive every one that is indebted to us. And lead us not into temptation; but deliver us from evil.
Luke 11:1-4

These things I have spoken unto you, that in me ye might have peace. In the world ye shall have tribulation: but be of good cheer; I have overcome the world.
John 16:33

It has been proven that everyone with

a prayer and fasting life prevails against any temptation in life. Trials and temptation will come in life, but as long as we have a prayer and fasting life, we will easily prevail against it. *"There hath no temptation taken you but such as is common to man: but God is faithful, who will not suffer you to be tempted above that ye are able; but will with the temptation also make a way to escape, that ye may be able to bear it."* (1 Corinthians 10:13)

In this race of life challenges and attacks, news of terror and tribulations will come to us. But as long as we have a prayer life, we will overcome all those temptations. *"For whatsoever is born of God overcometh the world: and this is the victory that overcometh the world, even our faith. Who is he that overcometh the world, but he that believeth that Jesus is the Son of God?"* (1 John 5:4-5)

THE LIFESTYLE OF PRAYER & FASTING IS A COMMANDMENT OF GOD

"Is not this the fast that I have chosen? to loose the bands of wickedness, to undo the heavy burdens, and to let the oppressed go free, and that ye break every yoke?" (Isaiah 58:6)

Chapter 1 What Is the Lifestyle of Prayer?

We are warned and instructed on what to do when we do fast and pray. Often some folks think that when they fast, they are fasting because the pastor said so—so they let him know how they did it. Others take fasting and prayer for a show and to let everybody know that they fast and pray on such and such day. We are commanded by the scripture below:

Moreover when ye fast, be not,
as the hypocrites, of a sad countenance:
for they disfigure their faces that
they may appear unto men to fast.
Verily I say unto you, They have their reward.
But thou, when thou fastest, anoint thine head,
and wash thy face; That thou appear not
unto men to fast, but unto thy Father
which is in secret: and thy Father, which seeth
in secret, shall reward thee openly.
Matthew 6:16-18

Our spiritual walk is not perfected without the incorporation of prayer and fasting as our lifestyle. It is mandatory for every believer who truly desires to witness His power and glory. *"O God, thou art my God; early will I seek thee: my soul thirsteth for thee, my flesh longeth for thee in a dry and thirsty land, where no water is; To see thy power and thy glory, so as I have seen thee in the sanctuary."* (Psalms 63:1-2)

The Holy Bible told us to pray and fast as long as we live. We must therefore embrace prayer and fasting as a lifestyle because it is a commandment of God. *"For this is the love of God, that we keep his commandments: and his commandments are not grievous."* (1 John 5:3)

EVERY TIME WE PRAY & FAST WE LAY UP TREASURES IN HEAVEN

But lay up for yourselves treasures in heaven, where neither moth nor rust doth corrupt, and where thieves do not break through nor steal: For where your treasure is, there will your heart be also.
Matthew 6:20-21

Among other recommended ways to lay up treasures in heaven in the Bible is the place of prayer and fasting. It is good be a cheerful giver and to do good to all that come around you. To help the poor and the orphans. To promote peace and live a righteous lifestyle. But if you do all this and eliminate prayer and fasting, you miss out on some vital heavenly treasures. Without prayer and fasting as a lifestyle you make your life vulnerable to the devil's attack.

PRAYER & FASTING GRANT US CONFIDENCE

When we develop a lifestyle of prayer and fasting, we secure heavenly faithfulness and confidence. Angels witness all we do—especially in prayers. Angelic help is not guaranteed until we have truly prayed. We receive the access key into the supernatural when we consistently pray concerning a prevailing challenge. Our mind becomes at peace concerning the prevailing challenges.

We are relieved every time we consciously pray and fast concerning any obstacle or prevailing challenge in life. Prayer and fasting give us assurance that God has heard our cry and our supplication. *"When I cry unto thee, then shall mine enemies turn back: this I know; for God is for me."* (Psalms 56:9)

THE DYNAMICS OF FASTING & PRAYER

The good news about prayer and fasting is that it reminds our spirit man that help and answers are on the way. Every time we consciously fast we are relieved of that prevailing predicament. When Daniel fasted for 21 days, an angel of God responded with an answer and told Daniel *"thy words were heard, and I am come for thy words."* (Daniel 10:12)

"Then said he unto me, Fear not, Daniel: for from the first day that thou didst set thine heart to understand, and to chasten thyself before thy God, thy words were heard, and I am come for thy words." (Daniel 10:12)

ONE DAY FASTING

Then all the children of Israel, and all the people, went up, and came unto the house of God, and wept, and sat there before the Lord, and fasted that day until even, and offered burnt offerings and peace offerings before the Lord.
Judges 20:26

The same way you fast for a whole day

to see your physician for a particular procedure, that is the same way we go before the Lord in fasting and prayer from early morning until evening to seek His face for answers. By recalling the above scripture, you will understand that a day fast is approved by the Holy Bible.

ABSOLUTE THREE DAYS OF FASTING

"And he was three days without sight, and neither did eat nor drink." (Acts 9:9) *"Go, gather together all the Jews that are present in Shushan, and fast ye for me, and neither eat nor drink three days, night or day: I also and my maidens will fast likewise; and so will I go in unto the king, which is not according to the law: and if I perish, I perish."* (Esther 4:16)

We are encouraged not to eat nor to drink in absolute fasting. Anyone seeking rapid and speedy answers from the Lord must engage in three days of fasting and prayer with sincerity. Every time we fast without prayer, it is not fasting. It is called a hunger strike. Fasting must be mixed with persistent intercession and supplication before God. We must pray from our spirit man until we get our desired answers.

21 DAYS OF FASTING

In those days I Daniel was mourning three full weeks. I ate no pleasant bread, neither came flesh nor wine in my mouth, neither did I anoint myself at all, till three whole weeks were fulfilled.
Daniel 10:2-3

These days most churches begin the year with this fasting method. Others do the 40 days fasting which Jesus and Elijah did in the Bible. Every time you are interceding for your community, a national crisis or for a country, we are encouraged to engage in 21 days of fasting and prayers.

BIBLE CHARACTERS WHO DEVELOPED SPIRITUAL MUSCLES BY FASTING

MOSES

"And he was there with the Lord forty days and forty nights; he did neither eat bread, nor drink water. And he wrote upon the tables the words of the covenant, the Ten Commandments." (Exodus 34:28)

Chapter 1   What Is the Lifestyle of Prayer?

Moses, the greatest prophet that ever lived, fasted for 80 days. This fasting secured not only the ten commandments, but also released the children of Israel from their Egyptians bondage.

APOSTLE PAUL

"In weariness and painfulness, in watchings often, in hunger and thirst, in fastings often, in cold and nakedness." (2 Corinthians 11:27)

The power behind Apostle Paul's ministry was fasting and total devotion to prayer unto God. Apostle Paul prevailed during all his challenges and obstacles because he was faithful to God in prayer and fasting. It is written: *"In weariness and painfulness, in watchings often, in hunger and thirst, in fastings often, in cold and nakedness."* (2 Corinthians 11:27)

DANIEL

"In those days I Daniel was mourning three full weeks. I ate no pleasant bread, neither came flesh nor wine in my mouth, neither did I anoint myself at all, till three whole weeks were fulfilled." (Daniel 10:2-3)

Although Daniel performed no known miracles during his lifetime, he prevailed and witnessed four presidents come and go because of his fasting and prayer life. The reason behind his excellent spirit was because Daniel was a man of fasting.

QUEEN ESTHER

"Go, gather together all the Jews that are present in Shushan, and fast ye for me, and neither eat nor drink three days, night or day: I also and my maidens will fast likewise; and so will I go in unto the king, which is not according to the law: and if I perish, I perish." (Esther 4:16)

Queen Esther prevailed and did not perish because of these three days of fasting and prayers.

JESUS

"And when he had fasted forty days and forty nights, he was afterward an hungred." (Matthew 4:2)
Jesus, to prevail against the devil's temptation, humbled himself to death because of this fast.

Remember...

Again, men like Moses fasted 80 days.

Chapter 1   What Is the Lifestyle of Prayer?

Elijah fasted 40 days. The early church fasted before going public worldwide. Most men of impact were men of prayer and fasting. Men like John Wesley, Jonathan Goforth, Jonathan Edward, DL Moody and Smith Wiglesworth, et. al., were all men of fasting and prayer.

There are no gimmicks in fasting and prayer. There is no mystical mystery or magic. Fasting means abstinence from food and water—depending on the instruction, as scripturally commanded and described. We punish and deprive our flesh—body—so that we can increase in the spiritual realm. We are humbled in the spirit, soul and body every time we genuinely fast and pray to God. God is seeking the humble, not the proud. *"The sacrifices of God are a broken spirit: a broken and a contrite heart, O God, thou wilt not despise."* (Psalms 51:17)

God resists the proud, but gives grace to the humble. Successful fasting and prayer must become a lifestyle if we are to prevail against the enemy. We incorporate the fruit of patience and endurance as a result of waiting on God. *"But they that wait upon the Lord shall renew their strength; they shall mount up with wings as eagles; they shall run, and not be weary; and they shall walk, and not faint."* (Isaiah 40:31)

A lifestyle of fasting and prayer grants us focus, determination and attention to detail. As often as we fast and pray, we observe, train our minds and teach our hearts patience and perseverance—especially in anticipation and expectation of what God promise He will carry out for us.

Fasting and prayer grants us access to hear directly from the throne of God and not from our church prophet or pastor. Fasting is an open access door to hear God's voice directly. We are always sensitive to proof of the spirit—as long as we pray and fast often.

BIBLICAL REASONS TO FAST

WE FAST FOR PROTECTION OF OUR LIFE AND PROPERTIES

Ezra the priest fasted for God's protection while carrying valuable things for God's temple. (Ezra 8:21-23) It is scripturally correct to fast and pray for protection.

Chapter 1   What Is the Lifestyle of Prayer?

FOR DELIVERANCE OF ANY NATION OR PEOPLE IN CAPTIVITY

Daniel fasted for the deliverance of the children of Israel from the ancient Babylonian captivity. (Daniel 10:3) We are encouraged to fast and pray—especially for the nations of Africa and the USA, not to mention the world at large. For satanic agents are at loose worldwide to inflict terror and pain on faithful believers. But we come against it in the name of Jesus.

TO FULFILL OUR CALLING & DESTINY

Jesus fasted to fulfill His calling and destiny in life. *"Being forty days tempted of the devil. And in those days he did eat nothing: and when they were ended, he afterward hungered."* (Luke 4:2)

When Jesus came out of this great fasting and prayer, He came back with power and authority for spreading the good news—the gospel. *"And Jesus returned in the power of the Spirit into Galilee: and there went out a fame of him through all the region round about."* (Luke 4:14) May you encounter such power to spread your name and calling, in the mighty name of Jesus. We are all called to God to fulfill specific significant mandates in our life. For us to accomplish our heart's desires and fulfill our destiny, we must embrace fasting and prayer as a lifestyle. *"And as he prayed, the fashion of his countenance was altered, and his raiment was white and glistering."* (Luke 9:29)

SUMMARY OF CHAPTER ONE

We Must Fast & Pray

As children of God, we cannot get things accomplished in life in the energy of the flesh. As believers, we must embrace fasting and prayer if we are to see new levels and breakthroughs on every side in life.

Remember...

Jesus spent 40 days to come out of the devil's temptation. *"Being forty days tempted of the devil. And in those days he did eat nothing: and when they were ended, he afterward hungered. And the devil said unto him, If thou be the Son of God, command this stone that it be made bread."* (Luke 4:2-3)

Elijah also spent 40 days in prayer and fasting to come out of depression and fear of Jezebel's threats. (1 Kings 19:8)

Chapter 1   What Is the Lifestyle of Prayer?

It is important that we incorporate prayer and fasting into our daily busy schedules. Godly wisdom demands that we devote to prayer discipline and subject our flesh into it as a ritual, daily dedicating our hearts into it as a daily routine.

WHAT IS THE LIFESTYLE OF PRAYER & FASTING?

Simply defined in my humble understanding, it is our ability to incorporate prayer into our lifestyle. It is the ritual and determination to devote quality time out of our busy schedule to pray as often as possible. If we eat three times a day, we can pray three times per day. I encourage you to determine to devote quality time to meet with God in prayer. If we are to succeed as Christians, we must incorporate prayer into our lifestyle.

DECISION KEYS

1) Nothing changes until you make up your mind.

2) Decision is the gateway to deliverance.

3) Until you decide, no one will decisde for you.

4) Your prosperity is proportional to your decisions.

5) The decision you make will determine the future you will create.

6) Decision creates future and fulfills destinies.

7) Decision beautifies our future.

8) Decision keeps you out of trouble.

9) Decision exempts you from evil.

10) Decision guarantees eternity.

Chapter 1   What Is the Lifestyle of Prayer?

11) You can only go far in life by your faith decisions.

12) You are poor because you made such decisions.

13) Make a decision and change your life.

14) Life-changing decisions are a function of quality information.

15) Success in life is a function of decision.

16) Life experiences are full of decisions.

17) Decisions change destinies.

18) Never settle for information—only look for revelation.

19) You are where you are today based on your last decision.

20) Information is crucial in decision-making.

21) Decision-makers rule the world.

22) You can rule your world by quality decisions.

23) As long as you decide rightly, Satan cannot harrass you.

CHAPTER 2

HOW DOES PRAYER & FASTING WORK?

The earnest, persistent prayer of a righteous man makes tremendous power available.
James 5:16 AMP

It is impossible to comprehend prayer without talking about faith. The simplest way that prayer and fasting work is by faith. Prayer and fasting work by faith. We must have faith in God. (See Mark 11:22.) We must also believe in God for prayer and fasting to work.

The opening scripture above used the word "persistent prayer of a righteous man." Unless we are determined to be "persistent," dedicated and devoted to prayer, we are not secured to witness testimonies. As you already know, prayer is the meeting place for us to speak to our Creator. If I am permitted to say it this way—prayer is the meeting place between humanity and divinity.

The answer to how prayer works is a mystery that cannot be understood in the energy of the flesh. Medical science and other men of research and scientific studies have always been curious to develop and propound theories on how prayer works. But may I submit to you that all their findings and theories have not answered the question—"How does prayer and fasting work?"

But as a humbled servant of God, may I submit to you that prayer is a mystery that we cannot comprehend with our physical understanding. We have to be in the spirit to understand prayer and fasting.

*But the natural man receiveth
not the things of the Spirit of God:
for they are foolishness unto him:
neither can he know them,
because they are spiritually discerned.*
1 Corinthians 2:14

Whenever we pray and fast, we are directly speaking to God—not to a man.

*For he that speaketh in an unknown
tongue speaketh not unto men, but unto God:
for no man understandeth him;
howbeit in the spirit he speaketh mysteries.*
1 Corinthians 14:2

Every time we engage genuinely in prayer and fasting, we provoke mysteries that cannot not be comprehended in the energy of the flesh. *"Call unto me, and I will answer thee, and show thee great and mighty things, which thou knowest not."* (Jeremiah 33:3)

WHAT ARE THE REWARDS OF PRAYER & FASTING?

CONFIDENCE

As we develop an attitude to totally depend on God, we develop confidence and assurance and peace of mind. Unless we walk in confidence, we will forever suffer defeat in life. Although self-confidence grants us victory in all things, it also boosts our spirit man. It boosts our belief system. *"And this is the confidence that we have in him that, if we ask any thing according to his will, he heareth us."* (1 John 5:14)

As praying men and women, we develop faith and become fearless against all adversaries, opposition and every challenge and obstacle in life.

> *For I know whom I have believed,
> and am persuaded that he is able
> to keep that which I have committed
> unto him against that day.*
> **2 Timothy 1:12**

Prayer gives us confidence and releases us from self-condemnation. *"The Lord shall fight for you, and ye shall hold your peace."* (Exodus 14:14) Every time we pray concerning a matter, we literally hand that case unto God.

HOPE

One of the greatest benefits of prayer and fasting is that it grants us hope without measure. It is easy to tell everybody about our travails and troubles, but we are not permitted to prevail until we tell God. Every time we pray concerning a prevailing trial or challenge, we are, to a higher degree, relieved of the worries and anxieties that trouble our mind.

Remember...

"For to him that is joined to all the living there is hope: for a living dog is better than a dead lion." (Ecclesiastes 9:4) Because we are joined to God in prayer, we develop hope that He will

answer us. It is written: *"But ye see me: because I live, ye shall live also."* (John 14:19)

It is written: *"Hope deferred maketh the heart sick: but when the desire cometh, it is a tree of life."* (Proverbs 13:12)

RESTORATION

Almost all over in the Holy bible whenever they fasted and prayed, God intervened with mighty restoration. Fasting is a short cut to restoration.

*If my people, which are called by my name,
shall humble themselves, and pray,
and seek my face, and turn from
their wicked ways; then will I hear
from heaven, and will forgive their sin,
and will heal their land.*
2 Chronicles 7:14

PRAYER & FASTING GRANT US SUPERNATURAL ENCOUNTERS

No one is permitted to experience power unless we pray and fast in life to a deeper degree. Not just pray and fast for two days or three days and then stop. The early church prevailed because of fasting and prayer. *"As they ministered to the Lord, and fasted, the Holy Ghost said, Separate me Barnabas and Saul for the work whereunto I have called them. And when they had fasted and prayed, and laid their hands on them, they sent them away. So they, being sent forth by the Holy Ghost, departed unto Seleucia; and from thence they sailed to Cyprus."* (Acts 13:2-4)

FASTING AND PRAYER BRINGS REVIVAL

If we are to experience personal revival, encounter God and hear from the angels of the living God, we must fast and pray. Fasting and prayer are powerful tools to provoke genuine revival in the life of anyone. Fasting and prayer cause the revival fire of God to fall upon us again. This revival fire grants us access into the fruit of the Spirit—love, joy, peace, patience, kindness, goodness, faithfulness, gentleness and self-control (Galatians 5:22)—but specifically the fruit of love, peace, righteousness and spiritual power over lusts of the flesh and the lies of the devil.

Chapter 2   How Does Prayer & Fasting Work?

GOD HONORS & ACKNOWLEDGES OUR FASTING & PRAYER

*A son honoureth his father,
and a servant his master:
if then I be a father, where is mine honour?
and if I be a master, where is my fear?
saith the Lord of hosts unto you,
O priests, that despise my name.
And ye say, Wherein have we despised thy name?*
Malachi 1:6

Many bishops, archbishops and high priests have made themselves God. Other foolish Christians have also followed suit. Unless we embrace fasting and prayer, God will not honor our prayers. The great deliverance pastor Derek Prince describes fasting as "a tremendous lesson in establishing who the master is and who the servant is. Remember, our body is a willing servant, but a terrible master."

"For the flesh lusteth against the Spirit, and the Spirit against the flesh: and these are contrary the one to the other: so that ye cannot do the things that ye would." (Galatians 5:17) The flesh, naturally, dominates our mind to be in control. But every time we fast, we humiliate our body and

exalt our spirit man.

Fasting and prayer convicts us to surrender our body to the trappings of the flesh and material world. Thus, by exalting the name of our Lord Jesus Christ, fasting takes us into a new dimension of a higher order, where we can hear quickly from the Holy Spirit. This allows us access into His presence—creating a refreshing spiritual atmosphere, stimulating us with joy and happiness.

WE MUST BE HUMBLE BEFORE GOD

In the Old Testament, fasting and prayer were the proven methods for the children of Israel to humble themselves. (Psalms 35:13, 69:10, Isaiah 58:5) God's people have always fasted to humble themselves, to receive cleansing of their sins by genuine and total repentance, forsaking their sins, for spiritual renewal and for special help. Ezra called a fast to seek God's protection for the Jews returning from Babylon to Jerusalem. (Ezra 8:21)

Chapter 2   How Does Prayer & Fasting Work?

WHY FAST AND PRAY?

*Howbeit this kind goeth not out
but by prayer and fasting.*
Matthew 17:21

There are some strange strong forces that will never give up on us unless we fast and pray. Unless we develop an attitude of prayer and fasting, we will never make an impact for the kingdom of God. The devil as the god of this world is a trickster who goes about harassing, torturing and tormenting weaker believers with old tricks in a new style or dimension.

"Be sober, be vigilant; because your adversary the devil, as a roaring lion, walketh about, seeking whom he may devour: Whom resist stedfast in the faith, knowing that the same afflictions are accomplished in your brethren that are in the world." (1 Peter 5:8-9) We established earlier that the devil is the god of this world.

In whom the god of this world hath blinded the minds of them which believe not, lest the light of the glorious gospel of Christ, who is the image of God, should shine unto them.
2 Corinthians 4:4

HINDERANCES TO PRAYER & FASTING

LACK OF FAITH

Our prayers and fasting must be mixed with our faith, otherwise it will be unproductive. *"But the word preached did not profit them, not being mixed with faith in them that heard it."* (Hebrews 4:2) Faith in God is the platform of prayer and fasting. Nothing gets done between us and Divinity until faith comes alive. *"But without faith it is impossible to please him."* (Hebrews 11:6)

It is written: *"And the apostles said unto the Lord, Increase our faith. And the Lord said, If ye had faith as a grain of mustard seed, ye might say unto this sycamine tree, Be thou plucked up by the root, and be thou planted in the sea; and it should obey you."* (Luke 17:5-10)

Lack of faith in God hinders our prayer and fasting. Every time we lack faith in God, our prayer and fasting is merely a hunger strike and a waste of our precious time. We must develop faith in God if we are to prevail in prayer and fasting.

Chapter 2 How Does Prayer & Fasting Work?

UNBELIEF

It is written: *"And he could there do no mighty work, save that he laid his hands upon a few sick folk, and healed them. And he marvelled because of their unbelief."* (Mark 6:5-6)

Unbelief is a destroyer of our precious destiny.

INIQUITY

Behold, the Lord's hand is not shortened, that it cannot save; neither his ear heavy that it cannot hear: But your iniquities have separated between you and your God, and your sins have hid his face from you, that he will not hear.
Isaiah 59:1-2

Iniquity means repeating a particular sin in your life, over and over again. As long as there is a sin that easily besets us, we will never prevail in prayer and fasting. *"Wherefore seeing we also are compassed about with so great a cloud of witnesses, let us lay aside every weight, and the sin which doth so easily beset us, and let us run with patience the race that is set before us."* (Hebrews 12:1) I admonish you, as you come out of iniquity, you will prevail in prayer and fasting, in supplication and in thanksgiving unto God.

WRONG INTENTION

Wherefore the Lord said, Forasmuch as this people draw near me with their mouth, and with their lips do honour me, but have removed their heart far from me, and their fear toward me is taught by the precept of men.
Isaiah 29:13

Oftentimes some of us think we can cheat on God. God does not look like man. God searches our heart. Until our heart is right with him we will never prevail in fasting and prayers.

Remember...

"For the Lord seeth not as man seeth; for man looketh on the outward appearance, but the Lord looketh on the heart." (1 Samuel 16:7)

It is written...

"And ye shall seek me, and find me, when ye shall search for me with all your heart." (Jeremiah 29:13)

God made it clear to us in this scripture

below that He searches our heart. "And God, which knoweth the hearts, bare them witness, giving them the Holy Ghost, even as he did unto us." (Acts 15:8)

It is written...

"I the Lord search the heart, I try the reins, even to give every man according to his ways, and according to the fruit of his doings." (Jeremiah 17:10)

Our intention must be right with God. We must be right with God and man before we can receive speedy answer from the exercise of prayer and fasting.

INWARD SIN

"For from within, out of the heart of men, proceed evil thoughts, adulteries, fornications, murders, thefts, covetousness, wickedness, deceit, lasciviousness, an evil eye, blasphemy, pride, foolishness: All these evil things come from within, and defile the man." (Mark 7:21-23) *"Now we know that God heareth not sinners: but if any man be a worshipper of God, and doeth his will, him he heareth."* (John 9:31) Bitterness, anger and all sin of the heart are evidence of wrong intention. Our God is a righteous

judge who will judge everyone accordingly.

"Great in counsel, and mighty in work: for thine eyes are open upon all the ways of the sons of men: to give every one according to his ways, and according to the fruit of his doings." (Jeremiah 32:19)

OUTWARD SIN

Now the works of the flesh are manifest, which are these; Adultery, fornication, uncleanness, lasciviousness, Idolatry, witchcraft, hatred, variance, emulations, wrath, strife, seditions, heresies, Envyings, murders, drunkenness, revellings, and such like: of the which I tell you before, as I have also told you in time past, that they which do such things shall not inherit the kingdom of God.
Galatians 5:19-21

We must genuinely confess and forsake our sins for us to prevail in prayer and fasting.

It is written: *"Know ye not, that to whom ye yield yourselves servants to obey, his servants ye are to whom ye obey; whether of sin unto death, or of obedience unto righteousness?"* (Romans 6:16)

We are all sinners. Every immoral thing you get excited doing is what makes you a sinner. *"Examine yourselves, whether ye be in the faith; prove your own selves. Know ye not your own selves, how that Jesus Christ is in you, except ye be reprobates?"* (2 Corinthians 13:5)

Although most faith people live in denial about the work of the flesh, from my own scriptural understanding everyone operating within the scope of Galatians5 :20-21 is classified as a sinner.

YOU MUST REPENT & CONFESS & PROCLAIM THE LORD JESUS CHRIST

The Word says, as many as received him, to them gave He power to become the sons of God. Even to them that believe on his name. To qualify for divine visitation, do the following sincerely:

1) Acknowledge that you are a sinner and that He died for you. (Romans 3:23)

2) Repent of your sins. (Acts 3:19, Luke 13:5, 2 Peter 3:9)

3) Believe in your heart that Jesus died for your sin. (Romans 10:10)

4) Confess Jesus as the Lord over your life. (Romans 10:10, Acts 2:21)

Now repeat this prayer after me:

Say Lord Jesus, I accept you today, as my Lord and my savior, forgive me of my sins wash me with your blood. Right now, I believe, I am sanctified, I am save, I am free, I am free from the Power of sin to serve the Lord Jesus. Thank you Lord for saving me. Amen.

Congratulations.

YOU ARE NOW
A BORN AGAIN CHRISTAIN!

Summary of Chapter 2:

Prayer and fasting will, for everyone—as long as we are willing to repent, confess and forsake our sins—humble ourselves before the Almighty God.

CHAPTER 3

THE BENEFIT OF PRAYER & FASTING

But thou, when thou prayest, enter into thy closet, and when thou hast shut thy door, pray to thy Father which is in secret; and thy Father which seeth in secret shall reward thee openly.
Matthew 6:6

OPEN REWARD

With reference to the above scripture, every time we pray we are promised that our Father, who sees in the secret, shall reward us openly. This open reward is not restricted on how it will come into our lives. It can come in any form, shape, style or time. Among open rewards of prayer are:

—Whenever we receive favor that we do not truly deserve.
—Whenever we are exempted from terror, attacks and torture.
—Whenever we receive financial favor, happy

marriage, breakthrough in business and career, job promotion, health and supernatural increase in every area of our life. We must therefore form a lifestyle of prayer and fasting for us to expect open reward from the Lord.

It is written: *"Moreover when ye fast, be not, as the hypocrites, of a sad countenance: for they disfigure their faces, that they may appear unto men to fast. Verily I say unto you, They have their reward. But thou, when thou fastest, anoint thine head, and wash thy face; That thou appear not unto men to fast, but unto thy Father which is in secret: and thy Father, which seeth in secret, shall reward thee openly."* (Matthew 6:16-18)

Prayer and fasting is voluntarily doing without food for our spirit man to be engaged with the spirit of the Lord. It is not compulsory that every time we pray we must also fast. We are not obligated to fast when we pray, but we must always pray whenever when ever we fast.

"But they that wait upon the Lord shall renew their strength; they shall mount up with wings as eagles; they shall run, and not be weary; and they shall walk, and not faint." (Isaiah 40:31)

Chapter 3   The Benefit of Prayer & Fasting

PRAYER & FASTING GRANTS SPEEDY ANSWERS

We must engage in prayer and fasting for speedy results in life. Every time we humble and subject our flesh before Him, He grants us speedy answers in our life. As believers, we must embrace praying and fasting, said Jesus.

PRAYER POINTS OVERCOME

Father Lord, deliver me from this present trial, in the name of Jesus.

1) Almighty Father, break me out of this present obscurity, in the name of Jesus.

2) Holy Spirit, help me to overcome this trial, in Jesus' name.

3) Holy Spirit, speak to me, in the name of Jesus.

4) Holy Spirit, minister to my subconscious spirit, in the name of Jesus.

5) Fire of God, burn down every mountain of difficulty, in the name of Jesus.

6) Holy Ghost, baptize me with your fire, in the name of Jesus.

7) Holy Spirit, go before me and favor me in this present challenge, in the name of Jesus.

8) Spirit of God, grant me liberty and freedom by the fire of the Holy Spirit, in the name of Jesus.

9) Father Lord, intervene on my behalf, in the name of Jesus.

10) Ancient of day, liberate me this season, in the name of Jesus.

11) Immortal redeemer, bring me higher above these prevailing changes.

12) Lord God, turn this present obstacale into my miracle, in the name of Jesus.

13) Fire of God, break down these obstacles for me, in the name of Jesus.

14) Holy Spirit, favor me in, Jesus' name.

15) Holy Spirit. release me from this challenge,

Chapter 3 The Benefit of Prayer & Fasting

in the name of Jesus.

16) Holy Spirit, become my compionion, in Jesus' name.

17) Holy Spirit, represent me in this matter.

18) Holy Spirit, elevant me beyond my own immagination, in the name of Jesus.

19) Holy Spirit, do not allow my enemies to truimph over my life, in the name of Jesus.

20) Fire of God, protect me, in the name of Jesus.

21) Fire of God, destroy my enemies, in the name of Jesus.

22) Fire of God, build a wall around me, in the name of Jesus.

23) Fire of God, expose my enemies, in the name of Jesus.

24) Fire of God, prove yourself, in the name of Jesus.

25) Holy Spirit, represent me in Jesus' name.

26) Holy Spirit, release your boldness into my life.

27) Holy Spirit, grant me signs and wonders.

28) Holy Spirit, make me a living wonder in my lifetime.

29) Holy Spirit, turn my life around, in the name of Jesus.

30) Holy Spirit, I will not remain at this level, in the name of Jesus.

31) Spirit of God, lift me higher, in the mighty name of Jesus.

32) Angels of God, minister unto me, in the name of Jesus.

33) Hand of God, separate me this season, in the name of Jesus.

Chapter 3   The Benefit of Prayer & Fasting

PRAYER POINT FOR PROTECTION

COVERING YOURSELF AND LOVED ONES FROM ATTACK

—It is written: *"Do not be afraid of sudden terror; nor of the trouble from the wicked when it comes; for the Lord will be your confidence. And will keep your foot from being caught."* (Proverbs 3:26)

—Therefore, O Lord, cover us and our loved ones from the activities of terrorists, in Jesus name!

—It is written: *"Avenge me of my adversary."* (Lk. 18:3)

—Therefore, O Lord, arise and avenge us of all my adversaries in the name of Jesus!

—It is written: *"They fought from the heavens; the stars from their courses fought against Sisera."* (Jud. 5:20).

—Therefore O heavens, fight for us in Jesus name!

—It is written: *"I will purge the rebels from among you, and those who transgress against Me; I will bring them out of the country where they dwell, but they shall not enter the land of Israel. They will know that I am the Lord."* (Ezek. 20:38)

—Therefore, O Lord, purge and sanitize our household in the name of Jesus!

—It is written: *"Then it was so, after all your wickedness—'woe, woe to you!' says the Lord God."* (Ezek. 16:23)

—Therefore, woe unto all the vessels that the enemy is using to do us harm in the name of Jesus!

—It is written: *"Behold therefore, I stretch out My hand against you, admonished your allotment, and gave you up to the will of those who hate you."* (Ezek. 16:27)

—Therefore, let our enemies be delivered into the hands of their enemies in Jesus name!

—It is written: *"You shall be for fuel of fire; your blood shall be in the midst of the land. You shall not be remembered, for I the Lord have spoken."* (Ezek. 21:32)

—Therefore, let all our spiritual enemies become fuel for divine fire in Jesus name!

—It is written: *"Then they will know that I*

am the Lord, when I have set a fire in Egypt and all her helpers are destroyed." (Ezek. 30:8).

—Therefore, O Lord, let all the helpers of our enemies be destroyed in the name of Jesus.

—It is written: *"And the people to whom they prophesy shall be cast out in the streets of Jerusalem because of the famine and the sword; they will have no one to bury them – them nor their wives, their sons nor their daughters – for I will pour their wickedness on them."* (Jer. 14:16).

—Therefore, O Lord, pour the wickedness of those who seek to destroy us upon their own heads in the name of Jesus!

—It is written: *"Call together the archers against Babylon. All you who bend the bow encamp against it all around; let none of them escape. Repay her according to her work; According to all she has done, do to her; for she has been poured against the Lord, against the Holy one of Israel."* (Jer. 50:29).

—Therefore, let all the hosts of the Lord turn against our spiritual enemies in Jesus name!

—It is written: *"Let God arise, let His enemies*

be scattered; let those also who hate him flee before him."* (Ps. 68:1)

—Therefore, O God, arise and let all your enemies in our lives be scattered in Jesus name!

—It is written: *"And He that searches the hearts knows what the mind of the spirit is, because He makes intercession for the saints according to the will of God."* (Rom. 8:27)

—Therefore, the intercessory prayers of Jesus, who is seated on the right hand of the throne of God, will not be in vain over our lives, in the name of Jesus.

—It is written: *"The Lord is your keeper; the Lord is the shade at your right hand. The sun shall not strike you by day, nor the moon by night. The Lord shall preserve you from all evil; He shall preserve your soul. The Lord shall preserve your going out and your coming in from this time forth, and even forevermore."* (PS. 121:5-8)

—Therefore, O Lord, spread your covering of fire and the blood of Jesus over us and our loved ones, in the name of Jesus.

—It is written: *"Rejoice always, pray without*

ceasing, in everything give thanks; for this is the will of God in Christ Jesus for you." (1 Thess. 5:16:18)

—Therefore, we thank you Father, for raising a spiritual shield over our loved ones and us. Thank you for giving us the heart for appreciating everything you are doing for us. Thank you for filling our hearts and our home with joy and peace that surpasses all understanding. Blessed be your name for all the answers to our prayers in the name of Jesus!

—You are holy, holy, Lord God Almighty, who was and is and is to come, Amen!

—O Lord, let our season of divine intervention appear in the name of Jesus!

—O you gates in the heavenlies standing against our destiny, lift up your heads in the name of Jesus!

—O you gates in the waters standing against our destiny, lift up your heads in the name of Jesus!

—O you gates in the earth standing against our destiny, lift up your heads in the name of Jesus!

—O you gates under the earth standing against our destiny, lift up your heads in the name of Jesus!

—O God, arise and destroy every gate keeper assigned against our lives in the name of Jesus!

—We break the backbone of every spirit of scarcity in our lives in the name of Jesus!

—O Lord anoint our eyes to see divine opportunities in the name of Jesus!

—Lord let every blindness to the treasures of our lives be cleared in the name of Jesus!

—Let our divine helpers appear in the name of Jesus!

—We declare, O Lord, that the rest of our lives will be better than the first part, in Jesus' name!

—We declare, O Lord that will overcome obstacles and defeat every enemy, in Jesus' name!

—We declare, O Lord that every blessing and promise that you put in our hearts will come to pass because this is our time for favour, in Jesus' name!

—We declare, O Lord that this is a new

Chapter 3   The Benefit of Prayer & Fasting

season of increase in our lives. We speak health, wisdom, creativity, divine connections and supernatural opportunities. They are coming our way, in Jesus' name!

—We declare, O Lord that we choose faith over fear. We are victorious in faith, in Jesus' name!

—We declare, O Lord that that we are not just surviving, this is our time to thrive in prosperity, in Jesus' name!

—We declare, O Lord that we will believe that we have received in the spirit even though we do not see anything happening in the flesh, in Jesus' name!

—We declare, O Lord that our rewards are being transferred to us because we remain in faith, in Jesus' name!

—We declare, O Lord that doubt will not ruin our optimistic spirit, in Jesus' name!

—We declare, O Lord that we are prisoners of hope and get up every morning expecting your favour, in Jesus' name!

—We declare, O Lord that you will do amazing things in our lives, in Jesus' name!

—We declare, O Lord that we are closer to

your abundant blessing than we think, our time has come, your promises will come to pass, in Jesus' name!

—We declare, O Lord that we will stay in an attitude of faith and expectation, in Jesus' name!

—We declare, O Lord that we are not worried, we know that you are our vindicator. It may seem to be taking a long time, but we will reap in due season if trust in you Lord, in Jesus' name!

—We declare, O Lord that you know the secret petitions our heart and we believe that they will come to fulfilment, in Jesus' name!

—We declare, O Lord that you will open new doors for us, in Jesus' name!

—We declare, O Lord that we will see your goodness, in Jesus' name!

—We declare, O Lord that this is our time to believe because favour is coming our way, in Jesus' name!

—We declare, O Lord that you have paved the way to abundant prosperity for us, prosperity more than we can every dream of or

imagine, for your sake, in Jesus' name!
—We declare, O Lord that in your eyes our future is extremely bright, in Jesus' name!
—We declare, O Lord that we will rise higher and higher and see more of your favour and blessings and we will live the prosperous life you have in store for us, in Jesus' name!
—We declare, O Lord that we may have a lot of turmoil, but we know that everything is going to be alright, in Jesus' name!
—We declare, O Lord that we have faith because we have put you first, in Jesus' name!
—We thank you, O Lord that our set time for favour is here, in Jesus' name!
—We declare, O Lord that our hour of deliverance has come, in Jesus' name!
—We declare, O Lord that there is no limit to what we can do, in Jesus' name!
—We declare, O Lord that there is no obstacle we cannot overcome, in Jesus' name!
—We declare, O Lord that that we have seen your accomplishments and they are good, in Jesus' name!

—We declare, O Lord that there is no challenge that is too great for us because you are with us, in Jesus' name!

—We declare, O Lord that you always succeed, in Jesus' name!

—We declare, O Lord that there is no financial difficulty or situation in our lives that is too great for you to resolve, in Jesus' name!

—We declare, O Lord that you are our Father Jehovah Jireh and that you own everything and you are our provider, in Jesus' name!

—We declare, O Lord that your promises declare that we are destined to live a victorious life, in Jesus' name!

—We declare, O Lord that we are your children, in Jesus' name!

—We declare, O Lord that the seeds of increase, success and promotion are taking a new root; your favour will spring forth in our lives in a great way; we will see new seasons of blessings and new seasons of your favour. It's our time to have abundant faith, in Jesus' name!

Chapter 3 The Benefit of Prayer & Fasting

—O Lord, it is written; according to your faith, it will be done unto you. Psalms 2:8 says *"Ask me and I will give you the nations as your inheritance."*

—Therefore, we ask you Lord to fulfil our highest hopes and dreams, in Jesus' name!

—We ask you this day, O Lord to give us our abundant blessing now, in Jesus' name!

—We dare to exercise our faith by asking you O Lord so that we may receive indeed, in Jesus' name!

—We thank you O Lord that for encouraging our faith, in Jesus' name!

—We declare, O Lord that this is our time for favour, in Jesus' name!

—We declare, O Lord that this is our time to prosper abundantly, in Jesus' name!

—We declare, O Lord that this is our time to have instant answers to prayer, in Jesus' name!

—We declare, O Lord that this is our time to ask and receive, in Jesus' name!

—We declare, O Lord that this is our time to thank you and testify for answered prayer, in Jesus' name!

—We declare, O Lord that we are blessed

and that goodness and mercy are following us right now, in Jesus' name!
—We declare, O Lord that you favour is surrounding us like a shield – you prosper us even in the desert, in Jesus' name!
—We declare, O Lord that you have great things for us in the spirit and that you have already released favour into our prayers, in Jesus' name!
—We declare, O Lord that you are a great and Holy God, in Jesus' name!
—It is written; delight yourself in the Lord and he will give you the desires of your heart (Ps 37:4).
—We therefore declare, O Lord that we delight in you because you are our Father God and because we are your children you have made us the head and not the tail. You want to take us to a new level of prosperity, in Jesus' name!
—We declare, O Lord that because we are your children, we are more than conquerors, in Jesus' name!
—We declare, O Lord that we are blessed and you supply all our needs. We have

Chapter 3   The Benefit of Prayer & Fasting

more than enough, in Jesus' name!
—We declare, O Lord that we have abundant favour indeed, in Jesus' name!
—We declare, O Lord that we are filled indeed with the presence of the Holy Spirit, in Jesus' name!
—We declare, O Lord that we have abundant faith indeed, in Jesus' name!
—We declare, O Lord that you have answered our prayers, in Jesus' name!
—We declare, O Lord that our debts are all paid up, in Jesus' name!
—We declare, O Lord that we are healthy, in Jesus' name!
—We declare, O Lord that we have no lack and that we have more than enough, in Jesus' name!
—We declare, O Lord that we are extremely blessed so much that we can bless your kingdom, in Jesus' name!
—We declare, O Lord that we are extremely blessed so much that we can bless others, in Jesus' name!
—We declare, O Lord that we have entered into an anointing of ease, in Jesus' name!

—We declare, O Lord that for every opportunity we have missed, every chance we've blown, you will turn the clock and bring bigger and better things across our path, in Jesus' name!

—We declare, O Lord that we will not settle for less than your best, in Jesus' name!

—Please restore the time that we have lost, O Lord that, in Jesus' name!

—Restore our victories, O Lord, in Jesus' name!

—Restore our lost joy, lost peace, lost health, lost insight, lost faith, lost dedication and desire to please you, we declare, O Lord in Jesus' name!

—We declare, O Lord that you use what was meant for our harm to our advantage, in Jesus' name!

—We declare, O Lord that you are a faithful God, in Jesus' name!

—We declare, O Lord that you will blossom our lives in ways that we can never imagine, in Jesus' name!

—We know, O Lord that you will bless us abundantly, in Jesus' name!

Chapter 3   The Benefit of Prayer & Fasting

—We know, O Lord that you will provide divine connections, in Jesus' name!

—We declare, O Lord that we are not suffering – we are blessed, in Jesus' name!

—We declare, O Lord that our difficulties will give way to new growth, new opportunities and new vision, in Jesus' name!

—O Lord let us see your blessing bloom in our lives in ways we would never dreamt possible, in Jesus' name!

—We declare, O Lord that we will stay in faith, so that what was meant to stop us will not be a stumbling block but a stepping stone taking us to a higher level, in Jesus' name!

—We declare, O Lord that we are not ordinary, but we are children of the most high God, in Jesus' name!

—We declare, O Lord that we created to rise above problems, in Jesus' name!

—We declare victory over strife O Lord, in Jesus' name!

—We declare, O Lord that no weapon formed against us shall prosper, in Jesus' name!

—We declare, O Lord that we are healthy and that no sickness shall live in us, in Jesus' name!

—We declare, O Lord that triumph is our birthright, in Jesus' name!

—We declare, O Lord that our setbacks are simply setups for greater comebacks that will place us to be better than we were before, in Jesus' name!

—We declare, O Lord that with you all things are possible, in Jesus' name!

—We declare, O Lord that we are in agreement with you. We know you have supernatural favour in store for us. You have supernatural opportunities, supernatural healing and supernatural restoration, in Jesus' name!

—We declare, O Lord that you want to do unusual things in our lives, in Jesus' name!

—We declare, O Lord that in faith, we have expectation deep in our spirits, in Jesus' name!

—We declare, O Lord that this will not be a survival year but a supernatural year in which you will abundantly come through

Chapter 3 The Benefit of Prayer & Fasting

for us, in Jesus' name!

—We believe, O Lord that you have come through for us, in Jesus' name!

—We declare, O Lord that because we hope in you, we will not be put to shame, in Jesus' name!

—We declare, O Lord that your word is right and true, you are faithful in all you do, in Jesus' name!

—We declare, O Lord that you are our refuge and strength, an ever present helper, in Jesus' name!

—We declare, O Lord that we will cast our cares on you and you will sustain us, you will never let the righteous fall, in Jesus' name!

—We declare, O Lord that you are the strength of our hearts and our portion forever, in Jesus' name!

—We declare, O Lord that you are our dwelling, therefore, no harm will befall us and no disaster will come near our tent, in Jesus' name!

—We declare, O Lord that you are our refuge and our fortress, in Jesus' name!

—We declare, O Lord that you will command your angels concerning us to guard us in all our ways, in Jesus' name!
—We declare, O Lord that even in darkness the light will dawn for us, in Jesus' name!
—We declare, O Lord that your word is eternal and stands firm in the heavens, in Jesus' name!
—We declare, O Lord that your faithfulness will continue throughout all generations, in Jesus' name!
—We declare, O Lord that you will keep us from harm; you will watch over our lives; you will watch over our coming and our going both now and for evermore, in Jesus' name! (Ps. 121)
—Thank you O Lord for the assurance that you are watching over us even when we sleep, in Jesus' name! (Ps. 13:5-6
—We declare, O Lord that you will drive those that do evil away from us and that you will protect us from their influence, in Jesus' name! (Ps. 66:1-4)
—We will shout with joy to you O Lord, we will sing the glory of your name and

Chapter 3   The Benefit of Prayer & Fasting

make your praise glorious. How awesome are your deeds! So great is your power that your enemies cringe before you, in Jesus' name!

—We declare, O Lord that that we will give you thanks for you answered us, in Jesus' name! (Ps. 118:21

—We declare, O Lord that we will praise you with all our hearts; before the gods we will sing your praise. We will bow down towards your Holy temple and will praise your name for your love and your faithfulness, for you have exalted above all things, your name and your word, in Jesus' name! (Ps. 138:1-3)

—You are holy, holy, Lord God Almighty, who was and is and is to come, Amen!

CONCLUSION

Howbeit this kind goeth not out but by prayer and fasting.
Matthew 17:21

All we have been saying is for us as believers to make prayer and fasting a lifestyle. It is inappropriate to neglect and ignore the place of prayer in our lives. We are not guaranteed to prevail in life until we embrace fasting and prayer as a lifestyle.

Literally, when the Bible says humble ourselves before the Almighty God and he will exalt us in due time, it was related to prayers.

"Humble yourselves therefore under the mighty hand of God, that he may exalt you in due time." (1 Peter 5:8)

Chapter 3   The Benefit of Prayer & Fasting

> *Let us hear the conclusion of
> the whole matter: Fear God,
> and keep his commandments:
> for this is the whole duty of man.
> For God shall bring every work
> into judgment, with every
> secret thing, whether it be good,
> or whether it be evil.*
> **Ecclesiastes 12:13-14**

All you have read remains a story until there is a quickening transformation inside of your heart. The mysteries of God are provoked only when you FEAR GOD and keep HIS commandments. The Bible says in Ecclesiastes 12:14—*"For God shall bring every work into judgment, with every secret thing, whether it be good, or whether it be evil."* If you are a born again Christian, we'd like to encourage you in your Christian life. If you are not a born again Christian, we can help you here receive genuine salvation. *"Therefore if any man be in Christ, he is a new creature: old things are passed away; behold, all things are become new."* (2 Corinthians 5:17)

Now repeat this prayer after me:

Say Lord Jesus, I accept you today, as my Lord and my savior, forgive me of my sins wash me with your blood. Right now, I believe, I am sanctified, I am save, I am free, I am free from the Power of sin to serve the Lord Jesus. Thank you Lord for saving me. Amen.

Congratulations.

YOU ARE NOW
A BORN AGAIN CHRISTAIN!

What must I do to determine my divine visitation?

To determine divine visitation you must be born again!

The word says as many as received him, to them gave He power to become the sons of God. Even to them that believe on his name.

To qualify for divine visitation, do the

following sincerely:

1) Acknowledge that you are a sinner and that He died for you. (Romans 3:23)

2) Repent of your sins. (Acts 3:19, Luke 13:5, 2 Peter 3:9)

3) Believe in your heart that Jesus died for your sin. (Romans 10:10)

4) Confess Jesus as the Lord over your life. (Romans 10:10, Acts 2:21)

Now repeat this prayer after me:

Say Lord Jesus, I accept you today, as my Lord and my savior, forgive me of my sins wash me with your blood. Right now, I believe, I am sanctified, I am save, I am free, I am free from the Power of sin to serve the Lord Jesus. Thank you Lord for saving me. Amen.

Congratulations.

YOU ARE NOW
A BORN AGAIN CHRISTIAN!

I adjure you to watch the Spirit of God and bear witness with your Spirit confirming His word with signs following. The Word says the Spirit itself beareth witness with our spirit, that we are the children of God. Join a Bible-believing church or join us on our weekly and Sunday worship services at 343 Sanford Ave., Newark, NJ 07106.

Chapter 3   The Benefit of Prayer & Fasting

WISDOM KEYS

— Every productive society is a society heading to the top.

—Millions of Nigerians run away from Nigeria. Very few Nigerians stay in Nigeria.

—My decision to return Nigeria is the will of God for my life.

—My shortcoming in America after 18 years is the fact that I've trained me to be wise, to think, reflect and reason appropriately.

—If you train your mind to reason, it will train your hands to earn money.

—It is absurd to use the money of the heathen to build the kingdom of the living God.

—Every ministry reveals its agenda and VISION either at the beginning or at the end.

—Be careful of your life. It is your first ministry.

—The average American mind is conditioned for a continual quest to get new things and discard the old.

—When I considered well, my BMW jeep became my initial deposit for the work of the ministry in Nigeria.

—Money will never fall from any tree or person. Make up your mind to be independent today.

—Everyone is waiting for you to change your mind. Until you change your thinking, nothing changes around you.

—Multiple academic degrees in other disciplines gave me the chance to think and reason.

—Whatever anyone is thinking at any time reveals what is inside of their heart.

—All planned events are the product of meditation.

—Every event is designed for a designated timeline.

—Wisdom is your ability to think, to create and invent.

—If you can think wisely enough, you will come out of debt.

—The distance between you and your success is your innovative and creative ability to think well.

—Success is the result of hard work, commitment, resolve and determined learning from past mistakes and failings.

—If you organize your mind, you have organized your life and destiny.

—There is a thin line between success and failure.

—Wealth is your ability to think, power is your ability to reason and success is your ability to be informed.

—If you can make use of your mind by thinking and reasoning, God will make use of your life and destiny.

—Reflect, reason, think and be Great.

—Famous people are born of woman.

—That you will make it is your intention, that you will survive is your resolve, that you will succeed with changes is your determination, personal efforts and hard work.

—No man was born a failure.

—Lack of vision is the result of failure.

—Working with mental patients encourages and aspire me to be a productive observant and dedicated to my assignment.

—Successful people are not magicians. It is the willpower, combined with hard work and determination and a resolve to succeed, that make them succeed.

—In the unequivocal state of the mind, intention is not a location or a position. It is the state of the mind.

—So many people think that they think.

Chapter 3   The Benefit of Prayer & Fasting

—The mind is used to think, to reflect and to reason.

—You will remain blind with your eyes open until you can see with your mind by thinking.

—There is no favoritism in accurate and precise calculation.

—Although knowledge is power, information is the key and gateway to a great future.

—It will take the hand of God to move the hand of man.

—With the backing of the great wise God, nothing will disconnect you from your inheritance.

—As long as you have wisdom and understanding of God, Satan and evil cannot manipulate your life and destiny.

—You have come this far in life by your own judgment and the decisions you made in the past. Now lean in and listen to God for another dimension of greatness.

—Great people are ordinary people. It is extra ordinary efforts and the price of sacrifice that produces greatness in them.

—As a mental direct care worker, I saw a great pastor and a motivational speaker within myself.

—A menial job does not reduce your self-worth. Until you resolve to achieve greatness and see greatness in all you do, you will never count in your community.

—The principle of Jesus will solve your gambling and addiction problems.

—The man of Jesus will lead you into heaven.

—Everyone has their self-appraisal and what they think about you. Until you discover yourself, other opinions about you will alter the real you.

—Supervisors and directors are just a position in the chain of command in a workplace. Never allow your supervisor hierarchy to alter your opinion of yourself.

Chapter 3   The Benefit of Prayer & Fasting

—Everyone can come out of debt if they make up their mind.

—The fact that I am not a decision-maker at work does not diminish my contribution to my world.

—Although it appears like it was a poor decision to accept a direct care employment at a psychiatric hospital, as I reflect on my nine years of that experience, it became apparent that I have learned and experienced enough for my next assignment.

—Self-encouragement and determination is a resolve of the heart.

—If you are determined to make a difference and do the things that make a difference, you will eventually make a difference.

—Good things do not come easy.

—Short cuts will cut your life short.

—Those who look ahead move ahead.

—Life is all about making an impact. In your lifetime strive to make an impact in your community.

—Make friends and connect with people who are moving ahead of you in life.

—If you can look around well, you have come a long way in your life, made a lot of difference and realized a lot of success in life.

—If you are my old friend, hurry up to reach out to me before I become a stranger to you.

—I am blessed with inspirations from God that changed my interpretation of the world around me.

—I thought I was stagnant and lonely until I looked around and noticed my children running around and my wife cooking.

—At 40, I resigned my job to seek the Lord forever.

—My ministry took a drastic rise to the top when the wisdom of God visited me with knowledge and understanding.

—You will be a better person if you understand the characteristics of your personality like your mood swings, attitudes and habits.

—It is the seed of love you sow into the heart of a child and a woman that you reap in due time.

—Love is not selfish. Love shares everything, including the concealed secrets of the mind.

—As long as you have a prayer life and a Bible, you will never feel lonely in the race of life.

—When good friends disconnect from you, let them go. They might have seen something new in a different direction.

—Confidence in yourself and in God is the only way to bring you out of captivity

—Never train a child to waste his or her time.

—The mind is the greatest asset of a great future.

—You walk by common sense, run by principles and fly by instruction.

—Those who become successful in life did it by self-determination, hard work and learning from past failures.

—Most successful people are lonely people. No one renders help to them, believing they are already successful. Except when they seek for more knowledge and information, they are all alone.

— I have seen a towing truck vehicle. I have also seen a towing ship in the water. But I have never seen a towing airplane in the air.

—I exercise my judgment and make a decision every minute of the day. Decisions are crucial, critical and vital with reference to your future.

—So many people wish for a great future. You can only work towards a great future.

—Your celebrity status began when you discovered your talent. What are you good at? Work at it with all your commitment.

Chapter 3   The Benefit of Prayer & Fasting

—Prayers will sustain you, but the wisdom of God will prosper you.

—When I met Oyedepo, his teachings changed my perspective. But when I met Ibiyeomie, his teachings changed my perception.

— I will be successful in ministry if only I concentrate and focus my energy in the work of the ministry.

— It took the late Dr. Norman Vincent Peale's book to open my mind towards the kingdom of success.

CHAPTER 4

PRAYER OF SALVATION

Neither is there salvation in any other: for there is none other name under heaven given among men, whereby we must be saved.
Acts 4:12

Are you saved? For you are not "SAFE" until you are "SAVED."

We encourage you to embrace the gift of salvation. Repent of any known sin in your life and live the remaining part of your life searching for God. Eternity is real—and hell is even more real. Therefore, I encourage you to repent, confess and forsake any known sin in your life and come with us as we follow the master—our Lord Jesus Christ.

What must I do to determine my divine visitation?

To determine divine visitation, you must be born again! The word says, *"As many as received Him, to them gave He power to become the sons of God. Even to them that believe on his name."* (John 1:12)

To qualify for divine visitation, do the following with sincerity—

1) Acknowledge that you are a sinner and that He died for you. (Romans 3:23)
2) Repent of your sins. (Acts 3:19, Luke 13:5, 2 Peter 3:9)
3) Believe in your heart that Jesus died for your sins. (Romans 10:10)
4) Confess Jesus as the Lord over your life. (Romans 10:10, Acts 2:21)

Now repeat this prayer after me:

Say Lord Jesus, I accept you today, as my Lord and my savior. Forgive me of my sins, wash me with your blood. Right now, I believe I am sanctified, I am saved, I am free. I am free from the power of sin, to serve the Lord Jesus. Thank you Lord for saving me. Amen.

Congratulations. You are now...

A BORN AGAIN CHRISTIAN.

Again I say to you—

CONGRATULATIONS!

I adjure you to watch the Spirit of God bear witness with your Spirit, confirming His word with subsequent signs. The word says, *"The Spirit itself beareth witness with our spirit, that we are the children of God."* (Romans 8:16)

Chapter 4   Prayer of Salvation

MIRACLE CARE OUTREACH

"...But that the members should have the same care one for another"
1 Corinthians 12:25

We are all members of the body of Christ. Jesus commanded us to love our neighbor as ourselves. This includes caring for one another as a member of one body. True love is expressed in caring and giving. The word says, for God so Love He gave....

Reach out to someone in need of Jesus. Help someone in crisis find Christ. Look out and prove your love to Jesus by caring and inviting your friends and associates to find Jesus the Healer.

Invite your friends to our Home Care Cell Fellowship (Miracle Chapel Intl. Satellite Fellowship). We're in the U.S. at 33 Schley Street, Newark, New Jersey 07112. Home Care Cell Fellowship Group meets every Tuesday at 6:00pm-7:00pm.

If you are in Nigeria—MIRACLE OF GOD MINISTRIES, aka "MIRACLE CHAPEL INTL." Mpama–Egbu-Owerri Imo state Nigeria.

LIFE'S NOT ALL ABOUT DURATION—IT'S ABOUT DONATION

What does this statement mean?

Life consists not in accumulation of material wealth. (Luke 12:15) But it's all about liberality…i.e., what you can give and share with others. (Proverbs 11:25) When you live for others, you live forever—because you outlive your generation by the legacy you leave behind after you depart into glory to be with the Lord. But when you live for yourself, when you are reduced to SELF—you are easily forgotten when you die and depart in glory.

Permit me to admonish you today to live your life to be a blessing to a soul connected to you today. I want you to know that so many souls are connected and looking up to you, and through you so many souls will be saved and rescued from destruction. Will you disciple someone today to find Jesus Christ?

As a genuine Christian, it is your duty to evangelize Jesus Christ to all you meet on your way. Jesus is still in the healing business—Jesus is still doing miracles, from time of old to now. Therefore, tell someone about Jesus Christ today, disciple and bring them to

Church. *Philip findeth Nathanael...* (John 1:45)

    Please prove the sincerity of your love for God today, please become a soul winner. The dignity of your Christianity is hidden in your boldness to proclaim and evangelize Jesus Christ to all you meet on your way. There is a question mark on the integrity of your Christianity until you become a life soul winner. Invite someone to join us worship the Lord Jesus this coming Sunday. Amen.

MIRACLE OF GOD MINISTRIES

PILLARS OF THE COMMISSION

We believe, preach and practice the following:

1) We believe and preach Salvation to every living human being.

2) We believe and preach Repentance and Forgiveness of sins.

3) We believe and preach the baptism of the Holy Spirit and Spiritual gifts.

4) We believe and teach Prosperity.

5) We believe and preach Divine Healing and Miracles—Signs and Wonder.

6) We believe and preach Faith.

7) We believe and proclaim the Power of God (Supernatural).

Chapter 4   Prayer of Salvation

8) We believe and proclaim Praise and Worship to God.

9) We believe and preach Wisdom.

10) We believe and preach Holiness (Consecration).

11) We believe and preach Vision.

12) We believe and teach the Word of God.

13) We believe and teach Success.

14) We believe and practice Prayer.

15) We believe and teach Deliverance.

These 15 stones form the Pillars of Our Commission. Become part of this church family and follow this great move of God.

MY HEARTFELT PRAYER FOR YOU

It is my burning desire for God to touch you through one of our teaching books or CDs. It is also my personal desire for you encounter God for yourself.

Now let me Pray for you:

I plead the precious blood of Jesus over your life. I decree and declare that no weapon fashioned against you shall ever prosper, every tongue that shall rise up against you God shall condemn it in judgement. From this day I declare your name in the lamb book of life. From this great day I declare goodness and mercy to hunt you down all the days of your life. Remain blessed, in Jesus name. Amen.

A MOMENT OF REFLECTION

We must always reflect on our lives. Have you ever considered what will happen to your soul the minute you depart into glory? Heaven is real therefore we must embrace righteousness, salvation, and repentance. God has promise that he will judge the wicked.

A greater portion of my ministry is to see you come to the knowledge of our Lord Jesus Christ. We must embrace the message of repentance and salvation. Listen to me today unless you are saved you are not safe.

It is written...

Keep thy tongue from evil, and thy lips from speaking guile. Depart from evil, and do good; seek peace, and pursue it.
Psalms 34:13-14

Just like the above scripture said...

We encourage you to do the following as you complete reading this book:

1) Guide your tongue. Watch what you say to yourself, to others and to the spirit of God.

2) Depart from evil. Repent and turn away from all appearance of evil acts, deeds, thoughts and desires.

3) Learn to do well. (Isaiah 1:17) Embrace righteousness as a lifestyle. Seek peace and pursue it .

CHAPTER 5

ABOUT THE AUTHOR

Rev. Franklin N. Abazie is the founding and Presiding Pastor of Miracle of God Ministries, with headquarters in Newark, New Jersey USA and a branch church in Owerri-Imo State Nigeria. He is following the footsteps of one of his mentors, the healing evangelist Oral Roberts of the blessed memory. The Lord passed Oral Roberts' healing mantle two days before he went to be with the Lord at age 91 into the hands of healing evangelist Rev. Franklin N. Abazie in a vision.

In all his services, the Power and Presence of God is present to heal all in his audience. Rev. Abazie is an ordained man of God, with a Healing Ministry reviving the healing and miracle ministry of Jesus Christ of Nazareth.

Pastor Franklin N. Abazie, has been called by God with a unique mandate: **"THE MOMENT IS DUE TO IMPACT YOUR WORLD THROUGH THE REVIVAL OF THE HEALING AND MIRACLE MINIS-**

TRY OF JESUS CHRIST OF NAZARETH.
"I AM SENDING YOU TO RESTORE HEALTH UNTO THEE AND I WILL HEAL THEE OF THY WOUNDS, SAID THE LORD OF HOST."

Rev. Abazie is a gifted, ardent teacher of the word of God, who operates also in the office of a Prophet, generating and attracting undeniable signs and wonders, special miracles and healings, with apostolic fireworks of the Holy Ghost. He is the founding and presiding senior Pastor of this fast growing Healing Ministry. He has written over 86 inspirational, healing and transforming books covering almost all aspects of divine healing and life. He is happily married and blessed with children.

Chapter 5   About the Author

BOOKS BY REV. FRANKLIN N. ABAZIE:

1) The Outcome of Faith
2) Understanding the Secret of Prevailing Prayers
3) Commanding Abundance
4) Understanding the Secret of the Man God Uses
5) Activating My Due Season
6) Overcoming Divine Verdicts
7) The Outcome of Divine Wisdom
8) Understanding God's Restoration Mandate
9) Walking In the Victory and Authority of the Truth
10) God's Covenant Exemption
11) Destiny Restoration Pillars
12) Provoking Acceptable Praise
13) Understanding Divine Judgment
14) Activating Angelic Re-enforcement
15) Provoking Un-Merited Favo
16) The Benefits of the Speaking Faith
17) Understanding Divine Arrangement
18) How to Keep Your Healing
19) Understanding the Mysteries of the Speaking Faith
20) Understanding the Mysteries of Prophetic Healing
21) Operating Under the Rules of Creative Healing
22) Understanding the Joy of Breakthrough
23) Understanding the Mystery of Breakthrough
24) Understanding Divine Prosperity
25) Understanding Divine Healing

26) Retaining Your Inheritance
27) Overcoming Confusing Spirit
28) Commanding Angelic Escorts
29) Enforcing Your Inheritance In Christ Jesus
30) Understanding Your Guardian Angels
31) Overcoming the Dominion of Sin
32) Understanding the Voice of God
33) The Outstanding Benefits of the Anointing
34) The Audacity of the Blood of Jesus
35) Walking in the Reality of the Anointing
36) Escaping the Nightmare of Poverty
37) Understanding Your Harvest Season
38) Activating Your Success Buttons
39) Overcoming the Forces of Darkness
40) Overcoming the Devices of the Devil
41) Overcoming Demonic Agents
42) Overcoming the Sorrows of Failure
43) Rejecting the Sorrows of Failure
44) Resisting the Sorrows of Poverty
45) Restoring Broken Marriages
46) Redeeming Your Days
47) The Force of Vision
48) Overcoming the Forces of Ignorance
49) Understanding the Sacrifice of Small Beginning
50) The Might of Small Beginning
51) Understanding the Mysteries of Prophesy
52) Overcoming Dream Nightmares

Chapter 5   About the Author

53) Breaking the Shackles of the Curse of the Law
54) Understanding the Joy of Harvest
55) Wisdom for Signs & Wonders
56) Wisdom for Generational Impact
57) Wisdom for Marriage Stability
58) Understanding the Number of Your Days
59) Enforcing Your Kingdom Rights
60) Escaping the Traps of Immoralities
61) Escaping the Trap of Poverty
62) Accessing Biblical Prosperity
63) Accessing True Riches in Christ
64) Silencing the Voice of the Accuser
65) Overcoming the Forces of Oppositions
66) Quenching the Voice of the Avenger
67) Silencing Demonic Prediction & Projection
68) Silencing Your Mocker
69) Understanding the Power of the Holy Ghost
70) Understanding the Baptism of Power
71) The Mystery of the Blood of Jesus
72) Understanding the Mystery of Sanctification
73) Understanding the Power of Holiness
74) Understanding the Forces of Purity & Righteousness
75) Activating the Forces of Vengeance
76) Appreciating the Mystery of Restoration
77) Overcoming the Projection & Prediction of the Enemy
78) Engaging the Mystery of the Blood
79) Commanding the Power of the Speaking Faith

80) Uprooting the Forces Against Your Rising
81) Overcoming Mere Success Syndrome
82) Understanding Divine Sentence
83) Understanding the Mystery of Praise
84) Understanding the Author of Faith
85) The Mystery of the Finisher of Faith
86) Attracting Supernatural Favor

MIRACLE OF GOD MINISTRIES

NIGERIA CRUSADE 2012

MIRACLE OF GOD MINISTRIES
NIGERIA CRUSADE
2012

MIRACLE OF GOD MINISTRIES
NIGERIA CRUSADE 2012

MIRACLE OF GOD MINISTRIES

NIGERIA CRUSADE

2012

MIRACLE OF GOD MINISTRIES

NIGERIA CRUSADE

2012

www.ingramcontent.com/pod-product-compliance
Lightning Source LLC
Chambersburg PA
CBHW021443080526
44588CB00009B/660